To

_____

From

_____

Date

_____

GREAT JOKES for EVERY GOLFER

Artwork by
Gary Patterson

Written by
Jeff Marion

HARVEST HOUSE PUBLISHERS

EUGENE, OREGON

GREAT JOKES FOR EVERY GOLFER

Text Copyright © 2010 by Jeff Marion
Artwork Copyright © by Gary Patterson

Published by Harvest House Publishers
Eugene, Oregon 97402
www.harvesthousepublishers.com

ISBN 978-0-7369-2603-4

Original illustrations by Gary Patterson. All rights reserved.

Design and production by Koechel Peterson & Associates, Inc., Minneapolis, Minnesota

Printed in China

10 11 12 13 14 15 16 / LP / 10 9 8 7 6 5 4 3 2 1

Dedicated to the Duffers
and Slammers, the Whiffers
and the Wagglers...
to all Golfers

GARY PATTERSON

To my wife, Lisa.
Thanks for putting up with
me and for letting me golf.

JEFF MARION

My ball spends so much time lying in sand traps it brings its own beach towel, suntan lotion, and umbrella.

The only sure method for improving your slice is to try a different pizza parlor.

One of the most important keys to a great game of golf is selecting the right club. Ideally, you want one you can fling at the nearest tree without hurting your shoulder.

When I'm teeing off, the safest place to stand is directly down the middle of the fairway. You won't get hit there.

The reason why golf is
so universally popular
is that it's socially
acceptable to be lousy at it.

Every golfer has a
handicap; mine is that I
was born without any
natural talent for golf.

According to USGA rules, you can improve your lie in certain situations. I improve mine every time I tell my buddies about the last round of golf I played.

Do you want to know the secret to a great golf score? Fuzzy math and a pencil with a good eraser.

A great way to improve your game is to emulate a pro like Tiger Woods. . . drink plenty of Gatorade and pump your fist a lot.

I'm not a golfer, but I play one on weekends.

If you are helping me look
for my ball out on the course,
here's a piece of advice.
Don't look in the hole or
anywhere on the green. You
won't find it there.

If the phrase "diamond in the
rough" is true, I'm going to be
a very rich man someday.

My definition of a good drive is the one I make in the cart to the clubhouse after my round is over.

I enjoy golfing in bad weather. I need as many excuses as I can get.

Golf is an expensive sport.
It will cost you the best
years of your life.

The closest I've ever come to a
hole in one was the time I bent down
too quickly to pick up my ball and
ripped my pants.

Good putting requires
intense concentration
and nerves of steel.
Unfortunately, my nerves
are held together with
bailing wire and two wads
of bubble gum.

Why is it that the worst golfer in the
group is always the one who takes
the longest to line up a putt?

They call golf a "gentleman's game," which may explain why I'm not any good at it.

There are no rules of etiquette regarding publicly loathing my very existence on the golf course, are there?

Other than the golf course or possibly speed dating, where else do you get 18 chances to humiliate yourself on the same day?

When swinging the club, remember to keep your head down. Even if this doesn't improve your swing, at least people won't be able to see who just made that awful shot.

As you get closer to the green, always aim for the flagstick—just make sure it isn't the one mounted on the roof of the clubhouse.

Golf is a game of etiquette. I'm always polite enough to leave the green wide open for the people I'm playing with rather than hitting my ball there.

What did I ever do to golf to make it hate me so much?

A lot of gambling takes place on the golf course—just look at what people are wearing.

What's the most nerve-racking task in all of golf? Trying to get all the range balls to fall perfectly into that little plastic bucket.

It's no coincidence that the two activities in life with the most rules are paying taxes and golfing.

I can easily drive the ball 300 yards. It might take me three holes to accomplish that, but I can definitely do it.

Golf is a lot like hunting. You spend all day waiting for that perfect shot, which may or may not ever materialize.

I prefer playing golf in the morning. . .before daybreak, when no one can see me and I don't have to pay to get on the course.

Let me introduce you to my very best friend out on the golf course. His name is Mulligan.

There are three inescapable truths in life: death, taxes, and the certainty I'll slice my drive off the first tee with everyone watching.

I'm not a bad golfer. I just enjoy the scenery on the course a lot longer than my playing partners.

7
110 YDS
PAR 2

Whoever came up with the phrase "practice makes perfect" definitely wasn't a golfer.

I have an incredible short game—short on talent, effort, and potential.

Golf pros will tell you to visualize the perfect swing before you address the ball. That's good advice. You want a nice mental picture in your head as you watch your ball sail into the neighboring fairway.

You know you're struggling with your golf game when your playing partners automatically yell "Fore!" before you've even finished your swing.

I hit my balls into the water so often that they have become SCUBA certified.

The divots I leave on the course are so large that if it rained and they filled with water, they could legally be declared wetlands.

They say golf is a good walk spoiled. I don't know about you, but when I go for a good walk, I don't typically drag a 20-pound bag around with me.

There's an excellent chance that someday I'll shoot a golf score that's under my age, provided I live to be a hundred.

They're making drivers bigger and better these days, which means I can hit the ball much farther into the woods than I used to.

Instead of cutting down our national forests, why don't they chop down the trees on the golf course so I can find my ball?

They called Jack Nicklaus "the Golden Bear," Greg Norman "the Shark," and Eldrick Woods, of course, "Tiger." If I had an animal nickname on the golf course, it would be "the Dodo."

Every aspect of my golf game is under par. . .except for my score, that is.

Golf is the only sport where you could make one good shot out of a hundred and still feel great about yourself at the end of the day.

How's my driving?
Call 1-555-NOT-GOOD.

I don't understand why people enjoy betting on the golf course. If I wanted to embarrass myself and lose money in the process, I would become a stockbroker.

My putting is so bad I need to enter a literacy program to read the green correctly.

One of the most important
components of your swing
is how you address the ball.
I've addressed the ball by
many different names. . .

A good sense of humor
is important when golfing.
All my playing partners seem
to have one. They spend the
entire round laughing at me.

If I had a nickel for every golf ball I've lost, the world's supply of precious metal would be severely depleted.

If you look at the best golfers in the world, they have one thing in common. They are not me.

Next to the golf course,
the only place I spend
more time in the sand and
water is at the beach.

You know the guy who ran into the bunker on the
17th hole during the Masters? That was me.

The only things I leave
shorter than my hair
are my putts.

My putting has really improved
since I started marking my ball
with a pizza pan.

Nothing compares to the feeling
of having played a really good round
of golf...or so I've been told.

If the game of golf
is 90 percent mental,
I definitely need therapy.